ARIZONA

NEVADA
UTAH
Lake Powell
Virgin R.
15
Lake
Mead
Grand Canyon
National Park
Colorado R.
Kingman
Bullhead
City
40
Big Chino Wash
Flagstaff
Little Colorado R.
Petrified Forest
National Park
40
40
Sedona
Chino Valley
Big Sandy R.
Lake Havasu
City
Prescott
Valley
Cottonwood
Prescott
Camp Verde
CALIFORNIA
Bill Williams R.
Sta. Maria R.
Alamo L.
17
Holbrook
Show Low
St. Johns
NEW
MEXIC
Parker
Colorado R.
Agua Fria R.
Verde R.
Payson
ARIZONA
10
Th. Roosevelt
Lake
Salt R.
White R.
Glendale
PHOENIX
Apache L.
Mesa
Globe
Black R.
Chandler
Maricopa
10
Gila R.
Casa
Grande
Florence
San Carlos
Res.
Gila R.
Gila R.
Yuma
San Luis
8
8
Coolidge
Clifton
Eloy
Safford
10
Marana
Oro Valley
San Pedro R.
Tucson
Saguaro
National Park
10
Sahuarita
19
Gulf of
California
MEXICO
Sierra Vista
Bisbee
Nogales
Douglas

ARIZONA

THE GRAND CANYON STATE

Jacqueline Hope Raynor

FIREFLY BOOKS

A FIREFLY BOOK

Published by Firefly Books Ltd. 2025

First Printing

Library of Congress Control Number: 2024947836

Library and Archives Canada Cataloguing in Publication
Title: Arizona : the Grand Canyon State / Jacqueline Hope Raynor.
Names: Raynor, Jacqueline Hope, author.
Description: Includes index.
Identifiers: Canadiana 20240494237 | ISBN 9780228105442 (hardcover)
Subjects: LCSH: Arizona—Guidebooks. | LCSH: Arizona—Description and travel. | LCGFT: Guidebooks.
Classification: LCC F809.3 .R39 2025 | DDC 917.9104/54—dc23

Published in Canada by
Firefly Books Ltd.
50 Staples Avenue, Unit 1
Richmond Hill, Ontario
L4B 0A7

Published in the United States by
Firefly Books (U.S.) Inc.
P.O. Box 1338, Ellicott Station
Buffalo, New York
14205

Cover and interior design: Jacqueline Hope Raynor
Photo Editor: Cathy Hoshino

Printed in China | E

FSC www.fsc.org MIX Paper | Supporting responsible forestry FSC® C160794

INTRODUCTION

Arizona has it all: hot summers and mild winters in the south, sweeping mixed forests, including the largest stand of evergreen ponderosa pine trees in the world, and breathtaking mountain ranges and snowy winters in the north. With just over seven million residents, Arizona is the 15th most populous state in the country and the population continues to grow due to the warm climate and attractive lifestyle choices.

Arizona was the last state of the lower 48 states to be admitted to the Union. Before the arrival of Spanish explorers, the area was occupied by a number of ancient Native American civilizations including the Hohokam, Mogollon, and Ancestral Puebloan cultures. Spanish explorers first arrived in 1539, and by the early 17th century, the Jesuits had established a series of missions across the entire southwest. As a result of the Mexican-American War (1846–1848), the area became part of the United States. It was first part of the Territory of New Mexico and then established as the Territory of Arizona, until Arizona joined the Union on Valentine's Day, 1912.

Notable places in the state include:

- The Grand Canyon, one of the world's seven natural wonders.
- The Four Corners, where Arizona, Colorado, New Mexico, and Utah touch.
- An abundance of wilderness areas, including Grand Canyon National Park, Saguaro National Park, and the unique Petrified Forest National Park.
- Hoover Dam, that provides electric power for Nevada, Arizona, and California.
- Taliesin West, Frank Lloyd Wright's winter home in the foothills of the McDowell Mountains.
- Ghost towns, including Tombstone, home of the O.K. Corral.
- Prehistoric cliff dwellings that provide a fascinating look into pre-European history.
- The Navajo Nation, the largest Native tribe in the country, with more than 300,000 citizens.

Stunning natural beauty, a mix of eclectic and vibrant cultures, and dynamic growing cities make Arizona a popular place to live and attract visitors from around the world.

(Previous page) **Horseshoe Bend is in Glen Canyon National Recreation Area, about 140 miles from both the Grand Canyon's North and South Rims. Around 5 million years ago the meandering rivers cut through the Colorado Plateau's layers of sandstone and created a roughly 1,000 foot deep, 270° horseshoe-shaped bend. Horseshoe Bend has become one of the most recognized and visited places in Glen Canyon.**

The Grand Canyon runs for over 277 miles across the northwest corner of the state. It is one of the most spectacular examples of erosion anywhere in the world. More than a mile deep, the canyon offers incomparable vistas from both the north and south rims. Grand Canyon National Park, over 1.2 million acres in size, offers visitors access to the canyon and the surrounding area.

(Left) Mather Point, with an elevation of over 7,000 feet, offers spectacular views of the South Rim of the Grand Canyon. On a clear day you can see for miles to the east and west and, looking down into the canyon, you can see portions of the Colorado River and the trails that crisscross the landscape. At the end of the day, visitors to the canyon are treated to some of the most glorious sunsets imaginable.

Right) Havasu Falls, located 20 miles east of Grand Canyon National Park, sits entirely within the Havasupai Indian Reservation. The falls are the most famous of the five aqua-blue Havasupai Waterfalls that spill over deep-orange, travertine cliffs creating a desert oasis of stunning beauty. The high concentration of calcium carbonate in the soil gives the water its blue-green color.

The Four Corners Monument (above) marks the point where the states of Arizona, Colorado, New Mexico, and Utah touch. This is the only place in the United States where the boundaries of four states meet. The boundaries of the states were established in the 1860s along meridian and parallel lines. By the beginning of the 20th century the monument had become a popular tourist destination.

Located in northeastern Arizona, Canyon de Chelly is owned by the Navajo Nation. Visitors are only allowed to travel in the canyons when accompanied by a park ranger or an authorized Navajo guide. Canyon de Chelly National Monument covers more than 83,000 acres and preserves ruins of the Indigenous tribes that once lived in the area. The park's most distinctive geologic feature, Spider Rock (left), is a sandstone spire that rises 800 feet from the canyon floor.

PLEASE DO NOT TOUCH!
NAVAJO RUGS

Hubbell Trading Post National Historic Site is located on Highway 191, north of Chambers. It is the oldest operating trading post on the Navajo Nation. In 1878 John Lorenzo Hubbell purchased the trading post and it continued to be run by the Hubbell family until it was sold to the National Park Service in 1967. The trading post is famous for its curated selection of authentic Navajo rugs and other southwest American Indian arts and crafts and exhibits of Navajo history and culture.

(Above) The Navajo Code Talker Monument is part of the Window Rock Tribal and Veteran's Memorial. During World War II over 400 Native American servicemen were employed as Code Talkers by the U.S. Marine Corps. Using Native American languages (Comanche, Hopi, Meskwaki and Navajo) they securely communicated vital information; their code was never broken.

(Right) Window Rock, made of soft Entrada Sandstone, which has been eroded to form the window, is a famous landmark located just north of the capital of the Navajo Nation, which is also named Window Rock. The Navajo Nation Museum, the Navajo Nation Zoo and Botanical Park, and the Navajo Nation Code Talkers World War II memorial are all located in Window Rock.

The world's largest Native American fair includes a rodeo, traditional Navajo music and dances, food booths, a Miss Navajo Nation Pageant, a parade, and an intertribal powwow. The Navajo Nation is the largest Indian reservation in the United States, comprising about 17 million acres, approximately the size of the state of West Virginia.

The Navajo Nation Fair has been held during the first week of September at Window Rock since 1948. It is a beacon of Navajo culture, attracting hundreds of thousands of participants and visitors.

Petroglyphs, like this Spanish Mural Panel at Standing Cow Ruin (above) near the town of Chinle, can be found in many of the parks in the state. The murals provide a fascinating glimpse into the very early settlement of the area by Europeans.

(Left) Hunts Mesa, home to West Mitten Butte, East Mitten Butte, and Merrick Butte, is a particularly beautiful rock formation within the Monument Valley Tribal Park. The valley's vivid red color is caused by the iron oxide that has been exposed as the siltstone weathered.

Lake Mead was created in 1936 with the completion of the Hoover Dam crossing the Colorado River. At full capacity, it can hold 9.3 trillion gallons of water; it is the largest reservoir in the United States in terms of water capacity. The dam controls the flow of water to the states of Arizona, California, and Nevada as well as some of Mexico. Lake Mead has been below full capacity since 1983 due to drought and increased water demand. The white mark on the rocks (or sides) is clearly visible because of the deposition of minerals on the rocks that were previously submerged.

(Left) Located in the Black Canyon of the Colorado River, Hoover Dam straddles the border of Arizona and Nevada. It is a major tourist attraction and receives over seven million visitors a year. Built during the Great Depression, the dam took five years to complete, and more than 100 workers lost their lives in the dangerous working conditions. As well as controlling the flow of water, the dam's generators provide electric power for public and private utilities in Nevada, Arizona, and California.

Established in 1991, the University of Arizona's Biosphere 2 is a research center located in Oracle. Originally built as a closed ecological system to explore the viability of prolonged human life in outer space, it remains the largest closed ecological system ever created. Currently, various research projects are underway here. The Biosphere hosts university and high school camps and is open for public tours.

Copper mining is a cornerstone of Arizona's history and economy. By 1910 the state had become the leading producer of copper in the United States. Morenci Mine is one of the largest copper producers in North America. Before officially adopting the nickname "Grand Canyon State," Arizona was also widely known as the "Copper State" because of the abundance of the mineral.

Jerome was a successful copper mining town until the 1950s when mining activities ceased and the population dropped from nearly 15,000 to under 100 people. Starting in the 1970s, the town has been resurrected as a tourist ghost town and artists' community.

TELEPHONE
TELEPHONE

Lake Havasu City was established in 1963 on the shore of Lake Havasu. Due in no small part to its desert climate and mild winters, it quickly became an active event destination for a wide range of activities, including the International Jet Sports Boating Association World Finals, fishing tournaments, custom boat regattas, and the Havasu Balloon Festival & Fair (above).

Originally built in the 1830s to span the River Thames in London, England, London Bridge (left) was disassembled, moved and reassembled in Lake Havasu City by Robert P. McCulloch, the real estate developer who founded the city. Since it opened here in 1971, London Bridge has become one of the top tourist attractions in Arizona.

When it opened in 1960 Sun City retirement community became an instant success. With a current population of just under 40,000 people, the hot, dry summers and mild winters of Arizona continue to attract retirees and snowbirds, residents of northern climates who relocate to warmer southern locales in the winter months. The community's unique street network design consists largely of concentric circles in four main pinwheels. Golf carts (above) are the preferred method of transportation for many residents and there are over 120 miles of golf cart paths within Sun City.

Kingman was founded in 1882 as a stop along the newly built railroad line between Winslow and Beale Springs. This railroad depot, built in 1907, was restored and reopened in 2011 as the Kingman Railroad Museum, featuring operating model train displays. Kingman is also home to the Arizona Route 66 Museum.

Oatman was a small mining camp until 1915 when two prospectors struck gold in the area. For the next decade the town was one of the largest gold producers in the American West. Mining operations were shut down in 1941 and Oatman became a virtual ghost town. Now a stop on the famous Route 66 nostalgia trail, the town feaures recreations of life in the Wild West, including wooden sidewalks and staged shootouts. But the true scene stealers are the wild burros roaming freely through the town, stopping traffic and nudging people for treats and attention.

(Left) The view from the Subway Cave in Boynton Canyon. Located close to Sedona, in Coconino National Forest, the hiking trails in the canyon are easily accessible and a popular tourist destination.

The Grand Canyon Caverns (above) are located just a few miles east of Peach Springs. Dry caverns are very rare, making up only three percent of the caverns in the world. Grand Canyon Caverns lie 210 feet below ground level and are among the largest dry caverns in the United States.

Planned as an artists' community and designed along the lines of a Mexican village, the Tlaquepaque Arts and Crafts Village, has been a Sedona landmark since the 1970s. Visitors can watch local artisans at work and visit galleries and boutiques that specialize in Southwestern art.

GALLERY

Slide Rock State Park, located in Oak Creek Canyon less than 10 miles from Sedona, is a popular vacation spot, attracting over 250,000 people per year. *USA Today* readers consistently vote Slide Rock one of the best swimming holes in the country.

Starting life as a private ranch, the beautiful Enchantment Resort in Sedona's scenic Boynton Canyon is now a 70-acre resort where visitors can enjoy biking and hiking trails and the relaxing spa offerings.

The Chapel of the Holy Cross is a Roman Catholic chapel nestled into the red rock buttes of Sedona at the base of a 1,500-foot-tall cliff. Built of sandblasted concrete, it was commissioned by local rancher and sculptor Marguerite Brunswig Staude and designed by August K. Strotz. Completed in 1956, the main feature is a 90-foot-tall iron cross on the southwestern wall. The chapel receives over two million visitors a year and is open for mass, confessions and weddings.

Hotel Monte Vista, built in 1927 and still operating today, is located in the historic downtown district of Flagstaff. Many famous people have stayed at the hotel, including Humphrey Bogart, John Wayne, and Spencer Tracy. Visitors may also encounter ghosts such as the "Phantom Bell Boy" who supposedly knocks on guests' doors in the middle of the night.

The Arizona Snowbowl ski resort (right), located a few miles outside Flagstaff, is a popular winter getaway that attracts close to 3,000 visitors a day during peak ski season.

(Previous page) Papago Park is a hilly desert park covering nearly 1,500 acres between Phoenix and Tempe. The park has many distinctive geological formations and a wide variety of desert plants, including the giant saguaro cactus, and is home to the Desert Botanical Garden, the Phoenix Zoo, the Arizona Heritage Center and the tomb of Arizona's first governor, George W.P. Hunt.

Hole-in-the-Rock of Papago Park (above), one of a number of openings erroded through the rock, is a popular tourist destination. Early inhabitants of the area are thought to have marked the passing of the seasons by marking the position of the sunlight shining through another opening in the top of the chamber.

(Right) Downtown Phoenix at dusk. Phoenix is the cultural center of Arizona and the most populous state capital in the country, with a population of over 1.5 million people.

The Legislative Governmental Mall or Wesley Bolin Memorial Plaza in Phoenix was established in 1978 by the Arizona Legislature. It is located across the street from the Capitol building and contains 30 memorials dedicated to individuals, organizations, and events, including World War I, World War II, the Vietnam War, the Korean War and Desert Storm. A monument to the United States Bill of Rights is believed to be the first erected to that purpose.

(Left) The Arizona State Capitol building in Phoenix was completed in 1901. Over the following decades additional buildings were added to house ever-expanding government departments. The original building is now maintained as the Arizona Capitol Museum with a focus on the history and culture of Arizona and includes exhibits featuring contemporary and historical artifacts from the Arizona state-owned collections.

City of Phoenix
City of Phoenix
City
Hall
200
City
Hall
200
MAIN ENTRANCE

(Left) Due to Phoenix's explosive growth, the Old City Hall, after several renovations and expansions, was finally replaced with a new building in 1994. The eye-catching modern building is 368 feet tall and has 20 floors. The Superior Court and the Maricopa County Justice Museum still use the Old City Hall.

(Above) The Desert Storm Memorial at Wesley Bolin Memorial Plaza commemorates the American-led liberation of Kuwait from Iraq in 1991.

Chase Field was opened in 1998. The stadium can seat over 48,000 people and is the home of Major League Baseball's Arizona Diamondbacks. It was the first stadium built in the United States with a retractable roof over a playing surface of natural grass. Following the introduction of a synthetic playing surface in 2019, the roof is kept mostly closed to reduce the strain on the HVAC system; Phoenix is the hottest major city in North America with game-time temperatures well above 100°F (38°C) during the summer.

(Right) State Farm Stadium in Glendale was originally known as University of Phoenix Stadium. It was renamed in 2018 and is the home of the Arizona Cardinals (NFL) and hosts the annual Fiesta Bowl. The stadium seats over 63,000 people.

22 ROGER WEHRLI
62 CHARLEY TRIPPI
ARIZON
CARDINA

The Heard Museum in Phoenix, founded in 1929, is dedicated to the advancement of American Indian art. The current collection contains over 40,000 books and artifacts. The Heard attracts 250,000 visitors a year and hosts a number of cultural festivals as well as art exhibits.

(Right) Tovrea Castle was completed in 1931 in a vernacular Italianate Architectural Style. Designed by Alessio Carraro, it was the private residence of E.A. and Della Tovrea. The castle is now part of the City of Phoenix Parks and Recreation Department, and the restoration of the building and surrounding park was completed in 2012. Nicknamed "The Wedding Cake Castle" by the locals, it is one of the most prominent landmarks in Phoenix and was added to the National Register of Historic Places in 1996.

The nonprofit Phoenix Zoo was opened in 1962 on 125 acres of land in the Papago Park area. From the beginning the zoo has been involved in conservation projects aimed at protecting endangered species and ultimately reintroducing them to the wild. With over 1,400 animals on display and several walking trails, it is a popular destination for residents and visitors to the city.

In 1937 Frank Lloyd Wright chose to build his winter home, Taliesin West, in the foothills of Arizona's McDowell Mountains in Scottsdale. The building was designed by Wright and his students, and built using timber, locally sourced stone, and concrete. Set harmoniously within the landscape with overlapping indoor and outdoor rooms, a triangular garden of native plants and a triangular pool, it showcases Wright's philosophy of "organic architecture." Taliesin West is now a World Heritage Site and a National Historic Landmark. It is the headquarters of the Frank Lloyd Wright Foundation and School of Architecture and is open for public tours.

In recent years Scottsdale has become one of the fastest growing cities in the United States. Its proximity to Phoenix, Tonto National Forest and the McDowell Mountains, as well as an influx of national companies offering employment opportunities, make it a popular place to live. Old Town Scottsdale is a favorite shopping destination.

Scottsdale's Museum of the West was established in 2015. The 43,000-square-foot building features exhibits chronicling the history, art and culture of the American West, Western Canada and Mexico. The museum is affiliated with the Smithsonian Institution and was selected as the Top Western Museum in the United States by *True West Magazine* in 2023.

FARGO

Mysteries and legends have swirled around the Superstition Mountains for as long as humans have inhabited the area, dating back to the time of the Pima Indians. Perhaps the most famous legend concerns the Lost Dutchman Gold Mine, which supposedly lies hidden somewhere in the Superstition Wilderness. Fortune seekers continue to search the mountains looking for the elusive mine but, so far, they have all come back empty handed. The Superstition Mountains are located east of Phoenix and tower more than 6,000 feet above the Sonoran Desert.

(Left) Apache Junction, located near Superstition Mountain, the westernmost peak of the Superstition Mountains, is named for the junction of the Apache Trail and Old West Highway. On Valentine's Day, 2004, Apacheland Movie Ranch was almost totally destroyed by fire; the Apacheland Barn (used in many Western films shot in Apacheland in the 1950s and 1960s) and the eye-catching white Elvis Chapel (left) are the last surviving structures and are cared for by the Superstition Mountain Historical Society.

In the summer of 1995 Elder Ephraim (a former abbot of Philotheou Monastery on Mount Athos, Greece) sent six monks to the southern Arizona desert near Florence. Their mission was to establish St. Anthony's Greek Orthodox Monastery in the name of Saint Anthony the Great, the father of monasticism. Today, the Holy Mountain, as it is called, consists of 20 independent monasteries, housing Orthodox Christian monks from across the world. Spanning almost 800 acres, with an elaborate system of gardens, citrus and olive groves, and gazebos with Spanish fountains, the monastery and its extensive grounds are an oasis in the desert. Visitors are welcome but there is a strict dress code.

Completion of the Tempe Town Lake (an artificial perennial reservoir) in 1999 allowed the rapid development of the surrounding area: office and residential highrises, a marina and a park that hosts numerous events throughout the year, as well as Mill Avenue, a popular shopping and entertainment area.

Tempe is the home of the main campus of Arizona State University. ASU Gammage, named for former ASU President Grady Gammage who commissioned his friend Frank Lloyd Wright to design the building, is a multipurpose performing arts center that hosts a wide variety of events. Completed in 1964, the building is considered to be one of Wright's last public commissions.

Yuma Territorial Prison in Yuma opened in 1876 and operated as a prison until 1909 when overcrowding led to inmates being relocated to a new facility in Florence. The building was then used as a high school, a hospital, a clubhouse and, during the Great Depression, homeless families lived in the cells. In 1961 the Yuma Territorial Prison State Historic Park opened to the public and is run as a historical museum by Arizona State Parks.

Cell Block Sponsor
Bruce & Debbie
Gwynn

With a population of over 500,000, Tucson is the second-largest city in Arizona and home to the University of Arizona. In the heart of the Sonoran Desert, the city boasts a wide range of museums, historic sites, hiking trails and golf courses. The Arizona-Sonora Desert Museum (above) contains some of the most unique flora and fauna in the world.

(Left) Tucson was built at the base of Sentinel Peak. In the 1910s, to celebrate their victorious football team, University of Arizona students used local basalt rock to construct a 160-foot-tall block "A" on the mountain's east face. Traditionally painted white, it has sometimes sported different colors such as green for St. Patrick's Day.

Spanish mission San Xavier del Bac, in Tucson, was begun in 1692. The building, erected by the Franciscans, was completed in 1797 and is the oldest European structure in the state. It is considered the most beautiful of the colonial churches established by Roman Catholic priests who moved northward from Mexico into Arizona. Today thousands of visitors make pilgrimages to the site.

At White Stallion Ranch in Tuscon, visitors can enjoy the cowboy lifestyle, one of Arizona's greatest experiences. Dude ranches, ranging from luxury resorts to bunkhouse living, offer visitors the chance to participate in seasonal horse drives, cattle roundups and rodeos.

Spread across 80 acres, the Pima Air & Space Museum in Tucson boasts one of the world's largest collections of historic aircraft. There are over 350 aircraft on display, ranging from vintage planes to iconic military jets and even retired commercial airliners.

0-20003
4748
151
U.S AIR FORCE
71433
386
25

Located mainly in the southeastern part of the state, fine wines from Arizona's vineyards have grown in popularity in recent years.

(Above) The harvest festival at Sonoita Vineyards, Elgin, offers fun for the whole family.

The Kitt Peak National Observatory is situated at the top of the almost 7,000-foot Quinlan Mountains on land belonging to the Tohono O'odham Nation. Guinness World Records lists them as having the largest gathering of major telescopes. The drive from the base provides some of the clearest mountain views in Arizona. The Nightly Observing Program telescopes reveal the desert sky's star clusters and shooting comets.

(Left) The annual All Souls Procession, inspired by the Mexican holiday *Dia de Muertos*, started in 1990 and has grown to attract over 200,000 people each year. Dressed in ornate costumes and carrying photographs and possessions of their loved ones who have died, participants march through the streets of Tucson to honor friends and family members they have lost over the years.

(Above) The Bird Cage Theatre is on Allen Street in the famous Old West Town Historic District, Tombstone. Notorious as a saloon and gambling hall, it is believed that at least 26 people died here; it is now a museum with more than 140 bullet holes still peppering the walls.

SPUR
WESTERN
WEAR

Built near the Goodenough Silver Mine, Tombstone quickly became the last boomtown on the American frontier. Most famous as the site of the gunfight at the O.K. Corral, the city celebrates its well preserved lawless past and is a popular tourist destination.

(Above) Boothill Graveyard in Tombstone contains at least 250 bodies, mostly outlaws. "Boothill" is a reference to the fact that a large number of the men buried here died violently with their boots on.

Meteor Crater is an impact crater west of Winslow, thought to be one of the best-preserved craters on Earth. Also known as Barringer Crater, it was created about 50,000 years ago when a meteor slammed into the earth. The crater was designated a National Natural Landmark in 1967.

The Painted Desert Inn, built in the Pueblo Revival Style is located within Petrified Forest National Park. The inn opened in the early 1920s and became a unique tourist attraction offering overnight accommodation. Severe structural damage and intermittent closures threatened the building with demolition, but it was saved by extensive and innovative restoration efforts. It became a National Historic Landmark in 1987 and is currently run as a museum.

Petrified Forest National Park is situated in Apache County and Navajo County in northeastern Arizona. The park spans 346 square miles and is named for its large quantity of petrified wood (fallen trees that lived in the Late Triassic Epoch, about 225 million years ago). Declared a national park in 1962, it receives over 500,000 visitors a year.

Cliff dwellings can be found in many of the region's parks and are a popular tourist destination. Tonto National Monument (above), in the Superstition Mountains, contains dwellings that were occupied by people of the Salado culture as early as the 13th century.

(Right) Montezuma Castle, located in Camp Verde was built by the Sinagua people. The eight-hundred-year-old, 20-room cliff dwelling, nestled into a towering limestone cliff is considered one of the best-preserved prehistoric cliff dwellings in North America.

The Tonto National Forest covers almost three million acres and is the largest of six national forests in Arizona. A popular wilderness destination, it is especially noted for unforgettable fall colors and the chance sightings of Salt River Wild Horses. Also known as mustangs, they are thought to be descendants of Spanish Colonial or Iberian horses brought to the Southwest by explorers in the 16th century. Approximately 300 horses roam across 20,000 acres of Forest Service land and are monitored by the nonprofit Salt River Wild Horse Management Group. Lucky visitors travelling down the lower Salt River can often catch sight of the horses when they come to drink and graze near the river.

PHOTO CREDITS

ALAMY

Rainer Lesniewski: 2; Hemis: 8; Efrain Padro: 9; Scott Warren: 13; Witold Skrypczak: 14; Russ Bishop: 15; Witold Skrypczak: 16; David South: 17; Hemis: 18; Hemis: 19; Janzig/USA: 21; Julie Quarry: 29; Westend61 GmbH: 30; Matthew Mawson: 31; BDP: 32; Richard Cummins: 33; RooM the Agency: 35; Charles Wollertz: 37; Craig Lovell / Eagle Visions Photography: 39; Ed Rhodes: 42; Luc Kordas: 43; Ian Dagnall: 52; morten Larsen: 53; Brenda Kean: 54; Michelle Jones – Arizona: 56; B. David Cathell: 58; Lightworks Media: 60; INTERFOTO: 62; Pat Canova: 67; Richard Cummins: 68; Richard Cummins: 69; Ian Dagnall: 72; Yvette Cardozo: 74; BIOSPHOTO: 75; Norman Wharton: 76; MERVYN REES: 77; Norma Jean Gargasz: 79; inga spence: 80; Buddy Mays: 81; Panther Media GmbH: 82; America: 90

SHUTTERSTOCK

Clari Massimiliano: 6–7; Ashley Hadzopoulos:10; iacomino FRiMAGES: 11; jejim: 12; Elena_Suvorova: 20; Steve Buckley: 22; Michael Vi: 23; Manuela Durson: 24; Jason Finn: 25; Hanna Steadman: 26; Ron Chilston: 27; NayaDadara: 28; JacobLoyacano: 34; Fotoluminate LLC: 36; Lissandra Melo: 38; Harry Beugelink: 40; Bill Perry: 41; Gregory E. Clifford: 44–45; Gregory E. Clifford: 46; Sean Pavone: 47; Sharon Ball: 48; Wangkun Jia: 49; Kit Leong: 50; Wangkun Jia: 51; Gregory E. Clifford: 55; JHVEPhoto: 57; Carrie A Hanrahan: 59; Joseph Hendrickson: 61; Raisa Nastukova: 63; Paul B. Moore: 64; Joseph Creamer: 65; Kristopher Kettner: 66; Sean Pavone: 70; BlueSky2U: 71; Traveller70: 73; DimaSid: 78; Gestalt Imagery: 83; Nick Fox: 84; Jeffrey M. Frank: 85; Dominic Jeanmaire: 86–87; Paul Brady Photography: 88; Juan Carlos Munoz: 89; Stephen Moehle: 91; Brent Coulter: 92; Richard Nantais: 93; Flaming Star: 96

INDEX

Beautiful spring pink cactus blooms in the Sedona desert.